LANDFALL

Landfall

Joe Denham

NIGHTWOOD EDITIONS

2017

Nightwood Editions
P.O. Box 1779
Gibsons, BC VON 1VO
Canada
www.nightwoodeditions.com

COVER IMAGE: "Three Houses Under a Dark Sky" by Peter Tucker
TYPOGRAPHY: Carleton Wilson

Canada

 Canada Council
for the Arts
Conseil des Arts
du Canada

 BRITISH COLUMBIA
ARTS COUNCIL
An agency of the Province of British Columbia

Nightwood Editions acknowledges financial support from the Government of Canada and the Canada Council for the Arts, and from the Province of British Columbia through the British Columbia Arts Council and the Book Publisher's Tax Credit.

This book has been produced on 100% post-consumer recycled, ancient-forest-free paper, processed chlorine-free and printed with vegetable-based dyes.

Printed and bound in Canada.

CIP data available from Library and Archives Canada.

ISBN 978-0-88971-336-9

CONTENTS

I: Poor Man's Rock   7

II: Landfall   33

III: Firestorm   55

...

Notes   73

Acknowledgments   75

About the Author   77

1: Poor Man's Rock

In the quiet that is the music of that place,
which is the difference between silence and windlessness.

—Jack Gilbert

Can we go then, without wilderness, within
windlessness, inside walls that won't

let the world in? The riot of rain
runnelling roads, whirling tires: the flooding

fires. And rot? The hard-moulded chemicals
will accumulate; will not. Will not you

work now: to leave; to love; to live
somehow beyond the seeming

(the seaming) ineptitude of thought?
Fuck the coin, the slot, the faux-

leather. The lever. The leavening
weather. Whether or not we.

Gathered as those unhoused, unhovelled, round
fire: the wire-bound, bridged and broken

city. Which owns me—inside this space
and time which loans me water (me:

water) and light (:and light), the blinding
white what's-to-come like a glacier-thick

wall of glass the present presses up against.
Unearthing the sun one thumb at a time—

once the final pelagic spawn sifts down
to the depths, dead as stone—stone within stone.

A home. A happiness. In light of.
And even so.

It runs clean through sleep across the seam
into the cardinal directions, the conquering

corners (from the filigreed, shadowed:
god's antechamber) to these all-too-

human arms. This murmuring heart.
A fish lost in a lost trap ghost-fishing

the ocean floor, circling and circling
the inner perimeter: the mind mapping

the mind's mirror image: time like a
tightening vice timelessness turns

its lightening to in the whitening next
-to-never, -to-ever: the pinpoint of lever.

Linking gravity and levity, rarity and
clarity, clasped. The last of the last

come so much more into focus gasping
on the verge of the extinction nexus.

Whittle your anger, it connects us. It
collects us. It corrects even those of us

who can't or won't hear the wind
coughing in the alders. The corporate

cornfields. And mountainsides of desertified
coniferous forest. It is the dream of

confluence without consequence. Without
care for what's causally taken. Awaken.

Beside the seashore as it rises and recedes,
on the leeside of desire and need.

And then the old-time agrarian ache amid
the age of home equity and agribiz

stocks moving up on earnings. The burnings.
So we'll sew our little seeds, come spring.

(Our little seeds, tucked and taped into torn
card-stock packets. *Safe as a toad in god's pocket.*)

Come spring. With swarms of starlings and
wasps on waves of light, with newborn breath

in the branches. With the ocean unteeming
(undreaming) now, with its corals withered white.

There came a stillness then, came also storm,
all of the oceans came. And I was wind-blind

and will be: weather-worn wind-shorn unwordly
on Poor Man's Rock. (No democracy no

illusory citizenry no art-not-*too*-heavy no strictly
competent poetry.) The mind expands

in the exposure, feeding like fire on air:
agnostic reverie, echolocation, grey sky

aswirl, dimming and torn. A stormwheel,
a veil: we're dreamed of and born, beloved.

We learn scorn. Learn otherness. Learn lies
to sing into the winds and the silences.

The stillness: that all our words of descent lie
impotent without the transposition of thought

into form. Each use of oil implicates. The veil
torn or untorn: it is *this* world we're decimating.

Give me a surface well, a hand-mill, a home:
by my own brow and back, stone upon stone.

Stone within stone: a happiness: love
grown strong in good ground, well sewn.

But the city sets the price, by the power-
pace (whether wired to the grid or lit

solely by fire, on principle). Burrow a hole
in its darkness, so the world might shine through.

And will. Because it's not windless and won't
be (it's inside you, inside me) and emanates

always from the echoless earth. The drum of
god in the ground. Every end's imminence.

The stories tell the seers stood white-blind
in the radiance: the further from, the closer

we come. Impermanence, that precious
precipice we wait upon, perched to fall.

I wore my hair shirt in the brittle morning
then went shopping at the mall. There's a stone

of truth and our world of lies inside. Inside us all:
the air we breathe still, with ease, assuming always.

With our wealth, these walls, wherein we
weaken our resolve, our resistance, our sense

and strength to live well within the wind
rain and stardust, sun and snow.

A shrouded follicle. A shelf of ice sliding
in slowmo to the sea seen in high resolution

on the sat-image viewing screen. The PowerPoint
projection. Which we watch without wonder

as with eyes at dusk, adapting to the darkening.
Meanwhile I am, you are, we are all self-

marketing. *Till rising and gliding out, I wander'd
off by myself in the mystical moist night-air...*

And from time to time looked up in perfect
silence at the stars. Though the silence is

ultimately imperfect, is perforated, is the
sound even of stone within stone being

ground by time down to down-drifting dust.
Which won't allow the simple repudiation

of knowledge by wonder: we're growing
darker. We're growing sunflowers high

over the asphalt driveway, carrot, zucchini,
squash and kale. The stars seem as though

screaming. Close, and teeming. It is
work enough, each day, to tend to and listen.

It's work enough to pay the bills, feed
the children, believe the future isn't

fracturing. What story shall we tell
ourselves this season? We all make

concessions. We all have our reasons.
Our reason: mind an extension of

my fingers, your feet, our collective sleep-
walking into walls. Our collective lack

of wherewithal. Yesterday's dodo is
today's flight path of our wireless

signals through the malignant neurons
in everything's brain. Tomorrow's refrain.

(THREADBARE)

Past and future, man's only riches.

—Simone Weil

If it's thought of, it's thought of as the delirium of fever wherein
    each breath of life

is rationed as light through a northern winter. If it's thought in,
    it's then and there.

Where it no longer matters your pleasure your panache your clever
    wit and clarity.

Inside that gravity and levity we are all infinite, indefinite: less and
    more. Infinitely

poor. When fever wakes you though awake you are already
    wavering within

what's taken or mistaken for a sense of god. Its presence.
    Or, it *is* presence.

So: the present tense. Light pooling at the back of sight,
   up-drifting. It could be

thought of as a plane, inward and outstretching: an umbilicus from
   us to timeless-

ness. No wonder we want dreamful sleep. And orgasm, ecstasy,
   catastrophe: any

catapult from time's tightened capillary out to its surrounding
   endless expanse.

Not the margins of pre- and post-existence, but the extant as noun,
   resistance,

the folding and folding of flowing fire into fire. Its burning blue
   clear centre.

Which won't be passed through as water won't be walked upon. Perhaps when the

light is gone, or gone to. But here the skin keeps the spirit encaged and the mind

enraged (if it's left to feel the world buckling under); the soul asunder. Poverty is

listening for the sound of rain's falling. Is trying to feel the Earth turn. Windburn.

In this time's scarcity and sadness, what's left us? The no-longer-opening hours.

The pillars of past and future fallen. The present a lintel over no door nor window.

And under no eaves nor gable. No load transfer to the footings of
before and after:

the dismantled structure unsituated, capitulated. Uncaptivated by
the vaulted

architecture, the complex veneer, how will we know when *when?*
is here? Nothing

in this world beyond sleep dreams clear. Its texture. Its tone.
Each exquisite

taste (of sex, of trembling timbre) in the inexpressible weather.
I know you want

just a little more, and deserve it so. And do. Adrift as we are inside
this open blue.

With no landmarks to set dead reckoning by. Nor stars. (When the
    gravity of what

we're doing, have done, becomes the only sun our darkened souls
    circle, will that then be

a suspended state of grace?) With but a trace the salmon
    the great auk the wild rye

gone. The old, sweet song unsung. I once strung a long rope
    upward from where I

rose each day—bewildered in sleep's fray—and held to it like
    a hard-fisted child

through the day. The weave unwound. Now hands clasped and
    harrowed, I pray.

Though not often. (And often only in fits of sadness or fear.)
    And with a somewhat

contrived countenance. So it seems nearly self-parody.
    (It's unhallowed, unholy.)

In my greatest weakness always I fall to my knees to the floor
    (in a squall of aware-

ness of frailty of impermanence). What is the colour of the light
    of the cold winter

air? I'll be in it past dark looking for the veil and the tear.
    Coddling, un/clear: this sin-

gular truth: with time it isn't a question of if (and space), but when
    and where. Out there.

Which is where/beyond? What's all this incessant seeking for
   what's known

otherwise as never-to-be-found? What, but the lowly feeble
   working-class ego

rattling the rancher window? Take the black mould stain coating
   the underside

of the roof, these walls which are carcinogen by composition
   as proof: I'll die

encumbered of all I can't cast off like a hook and line into air.
   Threadbare.

With feet unshod and face etched thin, by the unceasing wind
   I'll be taken in.

I'll be riven. A fissure like a fault line from my centre through
    which timeless-

ness will enter after time's engine (breath) unlights its fire.
    The moon in the cold

afternoon ghosted over the deepening blue: (that reflected white)
    we're not of our

own light. Though we adjust our staging, our sight, it's only with
    great volition

we capture and cast the slightest hint of some unknown sun.
    Like heat from stone

I'll open outward and relinquish it (to the emergent dark)
    what little light I was.

And I am *and* was (which is fetter and cause) oh so little
so sentient subliminally

poor. Lit like a child's nightmare by a night light in a hallway
through an open door.

At war with id and us and is. With the want for whiskey and whiles.
For miles and

miles of open road and the myth of everything cast off inside the
endless blue:

of everything, of anything, anew. We're untrue, utterly. And though
in time life renews,

it's this self-exemption, self-gain predilection that torques love
inward and ties.

All our lies laid bare, with god so near. Extinction is the poverty,
   is the sickness,

is the city of fear inside you and I, made clear. Everything in the
   elevated light of

what's left: the sorrow and the sacred; the suffering sea.
   With beauty so maligned

beyond the eye of the beholder (shoulder to shoulder at the
   world's wailing wall).

And hope, the heart's flail, despite the mind-scattering
   unfathomable destruction

exponential (lungless planet/lifeless sea); what has been, and will,
   by our will, be.

II: Landfall

here: this was history:
            their turn
                  is all they actually have
flowing in them.

—Jorie Graham

When we finally make landfall, when we torch the landfill or fall from the pedestal we're perched upon, precarious precipice: when the men and women who want war want war to end, send me a post-card with a picture of your god pinned to a corkboard and the word of your god etched in desert sand in the hand of the first witness to survive the filicide the genocide the twentieth-century Germans with their prisoners' liquid shit streaming down their legs dreaming of all the illegitimate children of each human species black brown yellow white red, the twenty-first-century and the night, the blessed, sacred, winnowing night, otherworldly, we slipped into everything: violence decay beauty: all the dead are with us in the breath: water and light and love was probably everything to the M-16-wielding child and the assholes on Twitter, bitterness the epicentre: which ism should we use as filter?

I hear the bats swift and almost silent, the firmament screaming: this was my idea of transcendence, a bottle of whiskey and a sweet slow fuck in a starlit field, the moon wandering the underworld, cave at the centre of my soul full of fungus-choked mammals, species upon species they're all disappearing: is there some reason we're all alone in this once-was-wonderful world?

Maybe if we squirrel away some money we can all chip in and start a fire, firestorm, bittersweet, the centre: enter stage right exit when we slump back into our devices—what would Francis Ponge have made of Pokémon Go?—did you notice a moment's pause in the to-and-fro fracas of all of us fucking this world to obituary and oblivion? If we step out into the world, the wind, without pretense or pretension, will we be growing anew or shedding our skin?

A sweet slow stoking, when we finally make landfall I'm going to eat dirt for seven days and empty the bowels of my brain into the howling exegesis. What we're now seeing: one-billionth of the spectrum of light, while we argue the dead and their story, the City injecting Roundup into Japanese knotweed, the children out back a' that there Wild West façade, on the slow drip, sugar and certainty; when did everything become facsimiles and variations on smug stupidity?

When we fall to our knees in a squall of awareness: the poisonous charters, insidious algorithms, corporations crawling across every synapse: mobile screen, dopamine, was it the driver or the pedestrian who wasn't looking?

When we finally run from the fallout of ourselves, the chemicals, every other species in a state of depensation, everywhere ground zero: a midwife and a coked-up banker walk into a bar—you write the punchline you barrel of laughs—there's too much history, all these happy firings-off of hip vacuity: is any of this art or is it all just Andy Warhol and haute couture? What if you had to choose between these easy aisles of cellophane and the future?

What if we actually have to choose?

There's a stage full of trust-funders singing the blues, it seems like everywhere the schmaltz is oozing, seeping through the cracks in everything, like there is no light shining, the seam is bursting, *How many rivers have we got to cross?* they're singing, all the minds of my generation capitulating, even the working poor, a plan for everyone, month to month or pay as you go, then gone: what are we now that we've bled and gutted song?

Ophelia, drugs are the only engine of survival: why do I always feel like I'm dying, slowly, and the moon no longer wanders my winter-mind: you wanted something beyond this small-town workaday hardscrabble, right?

See the frustration taking form in our children's forgotten joy: I'm going to count to three, you're going to exhale, and we're all going to smile.

We're going to make something, no doubt. Have you seen the sepia shots beamed back from the *Curiosity* rover? The wind laid the sand down so flat and thin you could almost reach in and crumble the cliffs with one godlike hand. And when we make landfall—long shadow of Olympus Mons—when we call the fossil record established, understood, understand that they stand under us, the fallen. When we walk hand in hand into every final burning horizon; they're almost forgotten, the great auk the salmon the wild rye, sentience: the sky is dimming, dust: didn't we leave something behind, something we were supposed to keep safe and close and cared for?

There's no more room for your sentimentality, no stars flaring against the green screen of your psychosphere, it's you yourself and the hammer you're holding pounding the world into submission, you and brother Jake and Osama and Mother Teresa, you're all on a mission from god or no-god, it makes no difference, makes us insular and old in the light of every new day that rises to our history: commerce, our particular liturgy: eat shit shop drive love hate repeat: this little piggy ate agribiz soy, this little piggy ate factory meat, this little piggy stood with that little piggy in the checkout line with fists full of money money money: land of milk land of honey, land that falls that fallows beneath concrete, corporations, incessant algorithms; beneath our never unshod, de-evolving feet.

Now the latest *fuehrer* is fodder for offhand humour, famine and etcetera *is* funny: absurdity a cage, a meme, an ocean we're sailing in a lucid dream across a wave pool with tidal simulation: wind rain barren-of-mind, hoist the jib the mizzen, put the ship in irons: *He is risen! He is risen!* zealots at the door with their pamphlets, their polyester, their whole other realms of idiocy. Cry me a river, a sea, an ocean of lost possibility. I'll make you fishers of men, make you slaves enough to fight wars for the rich, for this everyday horror: floor to ceiling plastic, floor to ceiling surveillance, floor to ceiling whatever we were searching for was forgotten somewhere in aisle five between stationery and oral hygiene, remember, you cracked that one about POTUS and his moobs and we were all doubled over in tears, laughing?

Full moon over the western hemisphere, white at the flame's centre—did you writhe deep in some archetypal ecstasy while you watched the revellers burn a bunch of shit down in the desert? There's a blackhole in the soul of your culture, all the land is unknowable, is unownable, is growing fallow; the farmers are in-theory, are questionable, dying their quotidian deaths, there's no way back (I used to wake in the night and implore time to untighten): what I wouldn't give for a clean glass of water, for an answer, for not just a liveable but a loving future.

It's trying to keep the floor under our feet that's escalating the urgency—unless we lift off, let go the tether: maybe we don't make landfall after all, maybe free will is a stone dropped forever into a bottomless well, kindness a curio in the collector's bone closet, of a fashion—what does curiosity really mean now that every stone's been overturned, now we're all guilty as charged and all the bodies are always and as-ever burning?

Because he says *there'll be a furnace on every street corner you'll see this is just the first loose stitch this election season you want change you'll get it* he says *the whole world's locked and loaded the white man he's always been good at shooting shit with guns ain't no putting him out to pasture fuck that there's a shit storm coming.*

Poetry? You've got to be kidding me.

What I want to do is lie to you so we can lie down together in this aftermarket dream, together, togetherness: it doesn't matter which side you're on, what matters is that you're on a side: far and wide the arms of dialogue and discourse and of course this is all just artifice— *You only kinda-sorta mean any of this, right, like, nobody breathing actually believes things are this hopeless?* The land isn't mine yours ours theirs its; the land isn't negotiating its stillness, its sacredness—it's a world apart from your consensus-factory-bureaucracy pedagogy, my polemic—simply breathing, as always, while we pound in iron pins and piss in every corner: war-commerce, history, our everyday horror, our every demanded apology.

I won't argue the point with you. I've been inside industry (a single bearing inside a great grinding machinery). We know money greases the wheels, we know it stops for nothing, it's intoxicating, each individual mind is incapably up-against; we all have our reasons, our rationale, I don't buy my own bullshit let alone yours: there are hours upon hours, the entire cosmos and every life I've taken with my own feeble hands, history: a cold heavy wind. I was trying to sing but the machines sucked me in: seated, eyes afire, thirst in every neuron, time in-wound, constricting the cells; the present a surging groundswell and we're seasick sailors puking our brains out on the aft deck of forever, no one left at the helm, no one left to hold course or even recall where it was we ever thought we were going—we can't hide in the mind, in the cloud of unknowing, all our religions our philosophies imagined before the awareness of extinction like a blossom, a kaleidoscope of butterflies in death-knell diapause— does anybody else want to just acknowledge the darkness here, in the amygdala, the dissonant chords we strike up for the dance, those old-trope fire-clouds on the far horizon gathering?

III: Firestorm

God is its howling.

—Paul Celan

To burn it down isn't a blazing torch
    isn't a riot
of flame afire, it's the open touch

of a hand in the poisonous soil
    mending. Fuck
Zeus in his flying fucking chariot,

right here is the world, the god, suck of
    the liveable now
exploding in our psychosphere. Luck,

and a happiness, a home: love grown
    good in good ground,
well sewn. Nobody's listening, wait for the tone:

Dear god, while you were lollygagging on high
    life made its mind
up on its own: *tentacular surround*

of the never-again, timebound, non-thought
    of human thinking:
pro-me/the us, unwound. Sure, the unkind

uncomely masses we are. Sure, the sink
    has a drain, has
a plug we can pull so the water swirls

down with the baby, with what we hold
    that's worth its weight
in everything taken: we've arrived sans

map sans compass (in love and hate
        and all that's become
of us) hauled by the pull of the ill-fate

we feel when the future looms near, future
        we pray for and
fear: what's coming is just a tiny bee flying

toward thee darling, a rollicking band
        of gypsies let's
join them why not why not ampersand

now? The golden calf the holy cow! All bets
        are off the burning's
inevitable: cast your gaze pull your nets

there's nothing left to kill to dwindle to lose
        anyhow. Death
is a window a door a wrong turn

full stop. Solipsist's a vibe killer.
        How 'bout *solip*
for a noun? Let's call down the grim reaper

on every corporate-stooge post-truth gossip-
        page fucker
still spouting the false promise of this war-

and-glitter economy, giving it hard
        to the world
three ways to Sunday while all the lovers

suffer in the mire. Bemoaning the Earth's
　　getting boring,
no? How 'bout we drink from the essence

of every lie we've ever told while yawning
　　ourselves to near-
sleep with our own self-delusion? The mooring's

let loose. Now we drift. Now we fear
　　we fret we
are utterly amiss. We've cried all the tears

till ours is tinder-dry anger, a sea of
　　flame unsailed upon:
let's burn down the box stores with song

(this feeble armchair pseudo-revolution)
　　let's be happy
and stale and unaccountably wrong.

That's our birthright, right, to be
　　better than most?
Let's raise a toast to the idiot, screen-drunk

masses: of course it's classless, the heavenly host
　　in Depends
and dollar-store reading glasses. Priority Post's

outmoded baby, you can insta-send
　　your tithe your
irrelevant opinion your banked-on

heckle from the peanut gallery, your
        right-on-cue
collusion. Even Jesus is a whore

in this post-everything curtain call
        take a bow take
take take, take one last look, adieu.

We are what we kill *and* what we make.
        The future is
yours! The future is distraction is fake

binary again binary, is fun. I took a whiz
        behind the bar
beneath the stars and all I could think of

was what a goof Purdy was. The bar
        so low was set
poets from both very near and far

let the whole enterprise go to shit.
        Who'd rather die
trying than roll over and live with it?

There must be a solace must be a sky
        must be a
chorus of questioners questioning why.

Let's each write a longform article
        on the reasons
we still live like it's the eighties, and how! A

survey of every excusatory exegesis:
    atheist, religious,
unhinged, holy cow: it's open season

on intuition and instinct, right and wrong
    and wow! WTF
are we doing, my love, where is god

in all this ransacking the sacrosanct? LOL
    did you just
say god again? Get over it dude! IMHO

your mind's like an old machine rusting
    in a rainstorm
ever falling. I know you must

know this, no? You don't need a weatherman
    to know which
way the wind blows, remember? This fire

scorches through, nothing's of our choosing:
    green flaring to
gold to the old broken ground. Throw a stitch

in time: nothing's sewn, nothing's saved. You
    wanted meaning
and love, *a life,* thought like the edge of a knife, new

modes of living, traditional basket weaving,
    a just footing
all tossed together somewhere over the mauve

horizon. But what we get is us: fallible, faulted,
    firestorming
through the world with *The goddess is alive and magic is afoot*

bumper stickers and prayers for a better world
    while we barely
manage to shop organic, resorting to carbon

credits to justify jet travel and our unsquare
    look into the eye
of who and what we are. The nearly

unseeable fading star of human dignity
    far off in
our electric-light-obliterated sky. What do we see

when we see *our* planet, *our* sea? Shark fin
    as food or
cause or low-swell panic, shark fin

as moral currency. How much more
    do you need,
do I? Not just the thing but everything

the thing offers as emblem, the seed
    the stem the fruit
the tree torched for warmth for credo

as effigy. Moral currency. Woot! Woot!
    Go humans
go! Off to work in your nice car nice suit

nice little pre-packaged preheated man-
        and-god-or-no-god
mantras. Meanwhile we fallow the humus,

the seven seas, wander this land of nod
        with a loop
of *What the fuck's going on here you stupid clod?*

running on repeat in our brains, a soup
        of perpetual shock
diluted with irony and apathy and a mélange

of assorted pharmaceuticals and stock
        footage advert
jingles and images making a mockery

of thought, of thinking that to subvert
        is to suffer
and fight for free will, freedom. The pervert

in me wants to just strip down and lather
        myself with KY
and whip cream and scream out like a mother-

less child into the endless, unbenevolent sky.
        I wanna get
really high on drug x and flat-out belie

everything about myself that seems to take
        take take
even though this world's but a silhouette

of its former form. If it *was* clear as a lake
   it's a murky pond
polluted by the unquestioned mistake

of progress without consequence, without
   care for what's
causally taken. We all know each of us is born

naked, warm and without blame, each of us a question
   to be answered
in the cold light that comes. And the fire, the rutted

landscape lit by our blaze and blast: swear
   faith to your
god as it rages through you: the caged swerve

in your id-drunk head, the cage's curve, encore
   encore bravo
the big fat phallus and the po-mo matador-

esque poet with his/her chest puffed: blow-
   hard barren-
of-mind, are you the shifting of the known

paradigm or just an art/i/fact of wellborn
   under-earned money?
(Though, sure: one more lithe phrase featuring winter wren

and I think I'll just find somewhere sunny
   to drink *cerveza*
por favor.) Damn right this is a war.

(And this an armchair, and this the savannah
          in the wilds of Botswana
where I can fly for a safari whenever I wanna.)

One more time tell me how you bought a
          sense of self
at the corporate bookstore, a sense of a-

theist certainty from the great wealth
          of science and
pop-ephemera philosophy, the one-half shelf

(life) of poetry from the homepage @www.bookland
          .com.
And then what? With all the answers on hand

you did proceed to Twitter and Facebook
          and Snapchat
and Tinder (why not get a #quickfuck

in there?) and disseminated from where you sat
          all wisdom and wonder
in digital form? Why raise the blinds? Why stand

for anything with everything asunder? The Saviour
          2000+® is coming
in VR. *Is* AI VR: is a world with more

sedentary distraction than the primitive lonely ever
          imagined. Seduction
is the perfect post and the million-Likes reaction. Tomorrow

is post-post-hope (pardon the pun): everything we'll ever want
    in pill screen neuro-exciter
form. Why resist? Why not conform like desire

swarming through the blood to the brain, to the sexual
    centre, animal, bestial, we're
made for each other, breakfast lunch dinner, amygdala

aflood with PEA, NE, DA and oh the omnipotent *Us*
    against the world against
the mob-stupidity and darkness. Hubris

the human condition, hubris the pat defiance
    and the easy acquiescence,
the lip service we pay love empathy (anti)war

poverty protest art democracy. Don't we all bow
    to the same god, this flooding
fire? In sickness, in silence, in despair: its presence:

not time, but what's underlying our dissimilar blood:
    mutual plunder, the pulsing
liminal pull in utero in situ *in medias res.* I could

swear I heard its howling upon waking, voice quavering
    beyond the margins of pre
and post, the extant everything that is and was, echoing—

without our hands, our hearts—into what will be.
    To burn it down isn't
a riot or righteous silence, isn't the clarion call of free-

dom ringing from streets forests seas—it's
        hearing the wind
and earth and water carrying, not the mystical void

but the manifestations, the near-inaudible song
        sweet and old
ringing through the ever-giving ever-living air:

this is reverence, a simple, knowable god:
        the cacophony
of utterances beyond the poisonous oversold

cities, world that sustains our maelstrom
        and malevolence, yet
keeps and loves us even so (if love be the spiracle

exhale of whales surfacing despite the violence
        of the centuries: now
and now they inhale, and sound, benevolence

in the endurance). We're bound today
        not by technology
but life's persistence, the present's

presence: what's left us—and left to us
        to choose.
To burn it down isn't the rising tide of progress

but a rising moon over an uncharted sea: lose
        the sense of being
human as other or beyond, god as chosen

in scripture story song; throw out every book
    written in the word
of certainty, step out to the edge and look

into the unset and unsettling world
    beyond your mind:
this little life we're hurled into

headlong, sinker-swimmers, we've lost
    ballast, bearing—
white-blind in the radiance—we've lost

clarity, that bright, unknowable shore.
    Here is the sextant,
here the oar. Here the limitless sea

we were taught to imagine in the slant
    light of solitude:
well-wrought lines, the door ajar on angular

thought, interrogative ad nauseam—dissimilitude
    strikes a wavering
match—each psyche aswim in the nude

simulacrum, everything a river
    aflood, overrun:
stomach spleen kidney lung liver

and a heart that loves, oblivion. Truth
    in the disillusion:
the gun the salesman the smarmy politician

unchosen. First there was breath. Then one
    zero one
zero one zero one: repeat till it's sung

over the old, sweet song, till it's
    undone.
Now the past is a questionable supernova

exploding to the super suck of now.
    We're bound
to each upon each (in time) but how:

you must know that everything lost isn't found
    by digging and digging
this old, petrified ground? Whatever we were seeking

someone just wanted kindness, a sprig
    of rosemary from
the garden in the gloaming light: spring

planting, summer harvest, northern sun.
    The sea scorched
hypoxic. See: the knot tied, the knot undone.

It happens so quickly. And carries on. Torch
    it down, it comes
surging forth, it comes: the open touch

of our small, living hands in the soil, rainfall
    from the still-giving
sky, forgiveness from no god but the evolving

world we're within: chance—perchance fortune—
    to love, to learn, to
try. We open our eyes to the given

day, which is all we have and is burning
    round and through:
here: this *is* history: our turn is

all we actually have flowing
    in us:
in-time, ever-burning, endless-blowing

windstorm landfall firestorm we
    live with and
within, trying to hold on to each other

as the future arrives—a window afire with
    sunlight, bedroom
walls aflame, bed where we lie together

loving and learning, always too soon
    leaving
into ourselves, memory, the future history

we share and face alone: stone within stone, death
    a lit
or blackened portal, otherworld or ending:

either way we're adrift and burning, firelight
    full in our darkening
eyes as they narrow to take in the flame.

The Jack Gilbert lines are from his poem "Music Is in The Piano Only When It Is Played."

"Safe as a toad in God's pocket," is John Thompson's phrase from "Ghazal xxxii."

"There came a stillness then, came also storm, / all of the oceans came," are lines from Paul Celan's poem, "There Was Earth Inside Them," translated by John Felstiner.

"Till rising and gliding out I wander'd off by myself, / In the mystical moist night-air, and from time to time, / Looked up in perfect silence at the stars," are lines from Walt Whitman's poem "When I Heard The Learn'd Astronomer."

The Simone Weil lines are from "Renunciation of Time," translated by Emma Crawford and Mario von der Ruhr.

The Jorie Graham lines are from her poem "Untitled," as is the phrase "tentacular surround of the never-again."

The Paul Celan epigraph is from his poem "Nocturne," translated by John Felstiner.

ACKNOWLEDGEMENTS

Thanks to the Canada Council for the Arts for financial support while writing this book.

To Jan Zwicky for her thoughts on some of these pages early on.

To Dennis Lee for his kind words.

To Silas and everyone at Nightwood Editions.

Thanks to Peter Tucker for the cover image, and to Wade Meisinger for help with the design.

This book—as it is a continuation of my previous work, *Windstorm*—is also to and for B.

Joe Denham is the author of four collections of poetry, including *Regeneration Machine* (Nightwood Editions, 2015) which won the Canadian Authors Association Award for Poetry and was nominated for the 2016 Governor Generals' Award for Poetry. Denham is also the author of a novel *The Year of Broken Glass*. His work has appeared in numerous magazines and anthologies including *Open Field: 30 Contemporary Canadian Poets*, (Persea, 2005) as well as *Spindrift* (Harbour, 2017). He lives with his wife and two children in Halfmoon Bay, BC.

PHOTO CREDIT: von Loewen